# THE LAND OF HEART'S DESIRE

# By WILLIAM BUTLER YEATS

A Digireads.com Book
Digireads.com Publishing

The Land of Heart's Desire
By W. B. Yeats
ISBN 10: 1-4209-4167-4
ISBN 13: 978-1-4209-4167-8

This edition copyright © 2011

Please visit *www.digireads.com*

## PERSONS IN THE PLAY

MAURTEEN BRUIN
SHAWN BRUIN
FATHER HART
BRIDGET BRUIN
MAIRE BRUIN
A FAERY CHILD

[*The scene is laid in the Barony of Kilmacowen in the county of Sligo, and at a remote time.*]

[*A room with a hearth on the floor in the middle of a deep alcove to the Right. There are benches in the alcove and a table; and a crucifix on the wall. The alcove is full of a glow of light from the fire. There is an open door facing the audience to the Left, and to the left of this a bench. Through the door one can see the forest. It is night, but the moon or a late sunset glimmers through the trees and carries the eye far off into a vague, mysterious world. Maurteen Bruin, Shawn Bruin, and Bridget Bruin sit in the alcove at the table or about the fire. They are dressed in the costume of some remote time, and near them sits an old priest, Father Hart. He may be dressed as a friar. There is food and drink upon the table. Mary Bruin stands by the door reading a book. If she looks up she can see through the door into the wood.*]

4

BRIDGET. Because I bid her clean the pots for supper
    She took that old book down out of the thatch;
    She has been doubled over it ever since.
    We should be deafened by her groans and moans
    Had she to work as some do, Father Hart;
    Get up at dawn like me and mend and scour;
    Or ride abroad in the boisterous night like you,
    The pyx and blessed bread under your arm.

SHAWN. Mother, you are too cross.

BRIDGET. You've married her,
    And fear to vex her and so take her part.

MAURTEEN. [*to Father Hart*]
    It is but right that youth should side with youth
    She quarrels with my wife a bit at times,
    And is too deep just now in the old book
    But do not blame her greatly; she will grow
    As quiet as a puff-ball in a tree
    When but the moons of marriage dawn and die
    For half a score of times.

FATHER HART. Their hearts are wild,
    As be the hearts of birds, till children come.

BRIDGET. She would not mind the kettle, milk the cow,
    Or even lay the knives and spread the cloth.

SHAWN. Mother, if only—

MAURTEEN. Shawn, this is half empty;
    Go, bring up the best bottle that we have.

FATHER HART. I never saw her read a book before,
   What can it be?

MAURTEEN [*to Shawn*] What are you waiting for?
   You must not shake it when you draw the cork
   It's precious wine, so take your time about it.

[*Shawn goes.*]

[*To priest*]

(There was a Spaniard wrecked at Ocris Head,
When I was young, and I have still some bottles.)
He cannot bear to hear her blamed; the book
Has lain up in the thatch these fifty years;
My father told me my grandfather wrote it,
And killed a heifer for the binding of it—
(But supper's spread, and we can talk and eat.)
It was little good he got out of the book,
Because it filled his house with rambling fiddlers,
And rambling ballad-makers and the like.
(The griddle-bread is there in front of you.)
Colleen, what is the wonder in that book,
That you must leave the bread to cool? Had I
Or had my father read or written books
There was no stocking stuffed with yellow guineas
To come when I am dead to Shawn and you.

FATHER HART. You should not fill your head with
   foolish dreams.
   What are you reading?

MARY. How a Princess Edain,
    A daughter of a King of Ireland, heard
    A voice singing on a May Eve like this,
    And followed half awake and half asleep,
    Until she came into the Land of Faery,
    Where nobody gets old and godly and grave,
    Where nobody gets old and crafty and wise,
    Where nobody gets old and bitter of tongue.
    And she is still there, busied with a dance
    Deep in the dewy shadow of a wood,
    (Or where stars walk upon a mountain-top.)

MAURTEEN. Persuade the colleen to put down the book;
    My grandfather would mutter just such things,
    And he was no judge of a dog or a horse,
    And any idle boy could blarney him;
    Just speak your mind.

FATHER HART. Put it away, my colleen;
    (God spreads the heavens above us like great wings
    And gives a little round of deeds and days,
    And then come the wrecked angels and set snares,
    And bait them with light hopes and heavy dreams,
    Until the heart is puffed with pride and goes
    Half shuddering and half joyous from God's peace;)
    And it was some wrecked angel, blind with tears,
    Who flattered Edain's heart with merry words.
    My colleen, I have seen some other girls
    Restless and ill at ease, but years went by
    And they grew like their neighbors and were glad
    In minding children, working at the churn,
    And gossiping of weddings and of wakes;
    For life moves out of a red flare of dreams
    Into a common light of common hours,
    Until old age bring the red flare again.

MAURTEEN. That's true—but she's too young to know it's
　true.

BRIDGET. She's old enough to know that it is wrong
　To mope and idle.

MAURTEEN. I've little blame for her;
　She's dull when my big son is in the fields,
　And that and maybe this good woman's tongue
　Have driven her to hide among her dreams
　Like children from the dark under the bed-clothes.

BRIDGET. She'd never do a turn if I were silent.

MAURTEEN. And maybe it is natural upon May Eve
　To dream of the good people. But tell me, girl,
　If you've the branch of blessed quicken wood
　That women hang upon the post of the door
　That they may send good luck into the house?
　Remember they may steal new-married brides
　After the fall of twilight on May Eve,
　Or what old women mutter at the fire
　Is but a pack of lies.

FATHER HART. It may be truth
　We do not know the limit of those powers
　God has permitted to the evil spirits
　For some mysterious end. You have done right.

　　　　　　[*To Mary*];

It's well to keep old innocent customs up.

[*Mary Bruin has taken a bough of quicken wood from a seat and hung it on a nail in the doorpost. A girl child strangely dressed, perhaps in faery green, comes out of the wood and takes it away.*]

MARY. I had no sooner hung it on the nail
    Before a child ran up out of the wind;
    She has caught it in her hand and fondled it;
    (Her face is pale as water before dawn.)

FATHER HART. Whose child can this be?

MAURTEEN. No one's child at all.
    She often dreams that someone has gone by,
    When there was nothing but a puff of wind.

MARY. They have taken away the blessed quicken wood,
    They will not bring good luck into the house;
    Yet I am glad that I was courteous to them,
    For are not they, likewise, children of God?

FATHER HART. Colleen, they are the children of the fiend,
    And they have power until the end of Time,
    When God shall fight with them a great pitched battle
    And hack them into pieces.

MARY. He will smile,
    Father, perhaps, and open His great door.

FATHER HART. Did but the lawless angels see that door
    They would fall, slain by everlasting peace;
    And when such angels knock upon our doors,
    Who goes with them must drive through the same storm.

[*A thin old arm comes round the door-post and knocks and beckons. It is clearly seen in the silvery light. Mary Bruin goes to door and stands in it for a moment. Maurteen Bruin is busy filling Father Hart's plate. Bridget Bruin stirs the fire.*]

MARY. [*coming to table*] There's somebody out there that beckoned me
And raised her hand as though it held a cup,
And she was drinking from it, so it may be
That she is thirsty.

[*She takes milk from the table and carries it to the door.*]

FATHER HART. That will be the child
That you would have it was no child at all.

BRIDGET. And maybe, Father, what he said was true;
For there is not another night in the year
So wicked as to-night.

MAURTEEN. Nothing can harm us
While the good Father's underneath our roof.

MARY. A little queer old woman dressed in green.

BRIDGET. The good people beg for milk and fire
Upon May Eve—woe to the house that gives,
For they have power upon it for a year.

MAURTEEN. Hush, woman, hush!

BRIDGET. She's given milk away.
I knew she would bring evil on the house.

MAURTEEN. Who was it?

MARY. Both the tongue and face were strange.

MAURTEEN. Some strangers came last week to Clover Hill;
　She must be one of them.

BRIDGET. I am afraid.

FATHER HART. The Cross will keep all evil from the house
　While it hangs there.

MAURTEEN. Come, sit beside me, colleen,
　And put away your dreams of discontent,
　For I would have you light up my last days,
　Like the good glow of the turf; and when I die
　You'll be the wealthiest hereabout, for, colleen,
　I have a stocking full of yellow guineas
　Hidden away where nobody can find it.

BRIDGET. You are the fool of every pretty face,
　And I must spare and pinch that my son's wife
　May have all kinds of ribbons for her head.

MAURTEEN. Do not be cross; she is a right good girl!
　(The butter is by your elbow, Father Hart.
　My colleen, have not Fate and Time and Change
　Done well for me and for old Bridget there?)
　We have a hundred acres of good land,
　And sit beside each other at the fire.
　I have this reverend Father for my friend,
　I look upon your face and my son's face—

We've put his plate by yours—and here he comes,
And brings with him the only thing we have lacked,
Abundance of good wine.
[*Shawn comes in.*] Stir Up the fire,
And put new turf upon it till it blaze;
To watch the turf-smoke coiling from the fire,
And feel content and wisdom in your heart,
This is the best of life; (when we are young
We long to tread a way none trod before,
But find the excellent old way through love,
And through the care of children, to the hour
For bidding Fate and Time and Change goodbye.)

[*Mary takes a sod of turf from the fire and goes out through the door. Shawn follows her and meets her coming in.*]

SHAWN. What is it draws you to the chill o' the wood?
There is a light among the stems of the trees
That makes one shiver.

MARY. A little queer old man
Made me a sign to show he wanted fire
To light his pipe.

BRIDGET. You've given milk and fire
Upon the unluckiest night of the year and brought,
For all you know, evil upon the house.
Before you married you were idle and fine
And went about with ribbons on your head;
And now—no, Father, I will speak my mind
She is not a fitting wife for any man—

SHAWN. Be quiet, Mother!

MAURTEEN. You are much too cross.

MARY. What do I care if I have given this house,
 Where I must hear all day a bitter tongue,
 Into the power of faeries

BRIDGET. You know well
 How calling the good people by that name,
 Or talking of them over much at all,
 May bring all kinds of evil on the house.

MARY. Come, faeries, take me out of this dull house!
 Let me have all the freedom I have lost;
 Work when I will and idle when I will!
 Faeries, come take me out of this dull world,
 For I would ride with you upon the wind,
 (Run on the top of the dishevelled tide,)
 And dance upon the mountains like a flame.

FATHER HART. You cannot know the meaning of your words.

MARY. Father, I am right weary of four tongues:
 A tongue that is too crafty and too wise,
 A tongue that is too godly and too grave,
 A tongue that is more bitter than the tide,
 And a kind tongue too full of drowsy love,
 Of drowsy love and my captivity.

[*Shawn Bruin leads her to a seat at the left of the door.*]

SHAWN. Do not blame me; I often lie awake
　　Thinking that all things trouble your bright head.
　　How beautiful it is—your broad pale forehead
　　Under a cloudy blossoming of hair!
　　Sit down beside me here—these are too old,
　　And have forgotten they were ever young.

MARY. O, you are the great door-post of this house,
　　And I the branch of blessed quicken wood,
　　And if I could I'd hang upon the post,
　　Till I had brought good luck into the house.

　　[*She would put her arms about him, but looks shyly at the priest and lets her arms fall.*]

FATHER HART. My daughter, take his hand—by love alone
　　God binds us to Himself and to the hearth,
　　That shuts us from the waste beyond His peace
　　From maddening freedom and bewildering light.

SHAWN. Would that the world were mine to give it you,
　　And not its quiet hearths alone, but even
　　All that bewilderment of light and freedom.
　　If you would have it.

MARY. I would take the world
　　And break it into pieces in my hands
　　To see you smile watching it crumble away.

SHAWN. Then I would mould a world of fire and dew
    With no one bitter, grave or over wise,
    And nothing marred or old to do you wrong,
    And crowd the enraptured quiet of the sky
    With candles burning to your lonely face.

MARY. Your looks are all the candles that I need.

SHAWN. Once a fly dancing in a beam of the sun,
    Or the light wind blowing out of the dawn,
    Could fill your heart with dreams none other knew,
    But now the indissoluble sacrament
    Has mixed your heart that was most proud and cold
    With my warm heart for ever; the sun and moon
    Must fade and heaven be rolled up like a scroll
    But your white spirit still walk by my spirit.

        [*A Voice singing in the wood.*]

MAURTEEN. There's someone singing. Why, it's but a child.
    It sang, "The lonely of heart is withered away."
    A strange song for a child, but she sings sweetly.
    Listen, Listen!

        [*Goes to door.*]

MARY. O, cling close to me,
    Because I have said wicked things to-night.

THE VOICE. The wind blows out of the gates of the day,
    The wind blows over the lonely of heart,
    And the lonely of heart is withered away.
    While the faeries dance in a place apart,
    Shaking their milk-white feet in a ring,
    Tossing their milk-white arms in the air
    For they hear the wind laugh and murmur and sing
    Of a land where even the old are fair,
    And even the wise are merry of tongue
    But I heard a reed of Coolaney say,
    When the wind has laughed and murmured and sung
    The lonely of heart is withered away

MAURTEEN. Being happy, I would have all others happy,
    So I will bring her in out of the cold.

*[He brings in the faery child.]*

THE CHILD. (I tire of winds and waters and pale lights.

MAURTEEN. And that's no wonder, for when night has fallen)
    The wood's a cold and a bewildering place,
    But you are welcome here.

THE CHILD. I am welcome here.
    For when I tire of this warm little house
    There is one here that must away, away.

MAURTEEN. O, listen to her dreamy and strange talk.
    Are you not cold?

THE CHILD. I will crouch down beside you,
    For I have run a long, long way this night.

BRIDGET. You have a comely shape.

MAURTEEN. Your hair is wet.

BRIDGET. I'll warm your chilly feet.

MAURTEEN. You have come indeed
    A long, long way—for I have never seen
    Your pretty face—and must be tired and hungry,
    Here is some bread and wine.

THE CHILD. The wine is bitter.
    Old mother, have you no sweet food for me?

BRIDGET. I have some honey.

    [*She goes into the next room.*]

MAURTEEN. You have coaxing ways,
    The mother was quite cross before you came.

[*Bridget returns with the honey and fills Porringer with milk.*]

BRIDGET. She is the child of gentle people; look
    At her white hands and at her pretty dress.
    I've brought you some new milk, but wait a while
    And I will put it to the fire to warm,
    For things well fitted for poor folk like us
    Would never please a high-born child like you.

THE CHILD. From dawn, when you must blow the fire ablaze,
You work your fingers to the bone, old mother.
The young may lie in bed and dream and hope,
But you must work your fingers to the bone
Because your heart is old.

BRIDGET. The young are idle.

THE CHILD. Your memories have made you wise, old father;
The young must sigh through many a dream and hope,
But you are wise because your heart is old.

[*Bridget gives her more bread and honey.*]

MAURTEEN. O, who would think to find so young a girl
Loving old age and wisdom?

THE CHILD. No more, mother.

MAURTEEN. What a small bite! The milk is ready now.

[*Hands it to her.*]

What a small sip!

THE CHILD. Put on my shoes, old mother.
Now I would like to dance now I have eaten,
The reeds are dancing by Coolaney lake,
And I would like to dance until the reeds
And the white waves have danced themselves asleep.

[*Bridget puts on the shoes, and the child is about to dance, but suddenly sees the crucifix and shrieks and covers her eyes.*]

What is that ugly thing on the black cross?

FATHER HART. You cannot know how naughty your words are!
That is our Blessed Lord.

THE CHILD. Hide it away,

BRIDGET. I have begun to be afraid again.

THE CHILD. Hide it away!

MAURTEEN. That would be wickedness!

BRIDGET. That would be sacrilege!

THE CHILD. The tortured thing
Hide it away!

MAURTEEN. Her parents are to blame.

FATHER HART. That is the image of the Son of God.
THE CHILD [*caressing him*] Hide it away, hide it away!

MAURTEEN. No, no.

FATHER HART. Because you are so young and like a bird,
That must take fright at every stir of the leaves,
I will go take it down.

THE CHILD. Hide it away!
    And cover it out of sight and out of mind!

*[Father Hart takes crucifix from wall and carries it towards inner room.]*

FATHER HART. Since you have come into this barony,
    I will instruct you in our blessed faith
    And being so keen witted you'll soon learn.

*[To the others.]*

We must be tender to all budding things,
Our Maker let no thought of Calvary
Trouble the morning stars in their first song.

*[Puts crucifix in inner room.]*

THE CHILD. Here is level ground for dancing; I will dance.

*[Sings.]*

The wind blows out of the gates of the day,
The wind blows over the lonely of heart,
And the lonely of heart is withered away.

*[She dances.]*

MARY. *[to Shawn]* Just now when she came near I thought I heard
    Other small steps beating upon the floor,
    And a faint music blowing in the wind,
    Invisible pipes giving her feet the tune.

SHAWN. I heard no steps but hers.

MARY. I hear them now,
    The unholy powers are dancing in the house.

MAURTEEN. Come over here, and if you promise me
    Not to talk wickedly of holy things
    I will give you something.

THE CHILD. Bring it me, old father.

MAURTEEN. Here are some ribbons that I bought in the town
    For my son's wife—but she will let me give them
    To tie up that wild hair the winds have tumbled.

THE CHILD. Come, tell me, do you love me?

MAURTEEN. Yes, I love you.

THE CHILD. Ah, but you love this fireside. Do you love me?

FATHER HART. When the Almighty puts so great a share
    Of His own ageless youth into a creature,
    To look is but to love.

THE CHILD. But you love Him?

BRIDGET. She is blaspheming.

THE CHILD. And do you love me too

MARY. I do not know.

THE CHILD. You love that young man there,
   Yet I could make you ride upon the winds,
   Run on the top of the dishevelled tide,
   And dance upon the mountains like a flame.

MARY. Queen of Angels and kind saints defend us!
   Some dreadful thing will happen. A while ago
   She took away the blessed quicken wood.

FATHER HART. You fear because of her unmeasured prattle;
   She knows no better. Child, how old are you?

THE CHILD. When winter sleep is abroad my hair grows thin,
   My feet unsteady. When the leaves awaken
   My mother carries me in her golden arms;
   I'll soon put on my womanhood and marry
   The spirits of wood and water, but who can tell
   When I was born for the first time? I think
   I am much older than the eagle cock
   (That blinks and blinks on Ballygawley Hill,)
   And he is the oldest thing under the moon.

FATHER HART. O she is of the faery people.

THE CHILD. One called,
   I sent my messengers for milk and fire,
   She called again and after that I came.

   [*All except Shawn and Mary Bruin gather behind the priest for protection.*]

SHAWN. [*rising*] Though you have made all these
    obedient,
  You have not charmed my sight and won from me
  A wish or gift to make you powerful;
  I'll turn you from the house.

FATHER HART. No, I will face her.

THE CHILD. Because you took away the crucifix
  I am so mighty that there's none can pass,
  Unless I will it, where my feet have danced
  Or where I've whirled my finger-tops.

  [*Shawn tries to approach her and cannot.*]

MAURTEEN. Look, look!
  There something stops him—look how he moves his
    hands
  As though he rubbed them on a wall of glass!

FATHER HART. I will confront this mighty spirit alone.
  Be not afraid, the Father is with us,
  (The Holy Martyrs and the Innocents,
  The adoring Magi in their coats of mail,)
  And He who died and rose on the third day
  (And all the nine angelic hierarchies.)

  [*The Child kneels upon the settle beside Mary and puts
  her arms about her.*]

  Cry, daughter, to the Angels and the Saints.

THE CHILD. You shall go with me, newly-married bride,
    And gaze upon a merrier multitude.
    (White-armed Nuala, Aengus of the Birds,
    Feacra of the hurtling foam, and him
    Who is the ruler of the Western Host,
    Finvaragh, and their Land of Heart's Desire,)
    Where beauty has no ebb, decay no flood,
    But joy is wisdom, Time an endless song.
    I kiss you and the world begins to fade.

SHAWN. Awake out of that trance—and cover up
    Your eyes and ears.

FATHER HART. She must both look and listen,
    For only the soul's choice can save her now.
    Come over to me, daughter; stand beside me;
    Think of this house and of your duties in it.

THE CHILD. Stay and come with me, newly-married bride,
    For if you hear him you grow like the rest;
    Bear children, cook, and bend above the churn,
    And wrangle over butter, fowl, and eggs,
    Until at last, grown old and bitter of tongue,
    You're crouching there and shivering at the grave.

FATHER HART. Daughter, I point you out the way to Heaven.

THE CHILD. But I can lead you, newly-married bride,
　　Where nobody gets old and crafty and wise,
　　Where nobody gets old and godly and grave,
　　Where nobody gets old and bitter of tongue,
　　And where kind tongues bring no captivity;
　　For we are but obedient to the thoughts
　　That drift into the mind at a wink of the eye.

FATHER HART. By the dear Name of the One crucified,
　　I bid you, Mary Bruin, come to me.

THE CHILD. I keep you in the name of your own heart.

FATHER HART. It is because I put away the crucifix
　　That I am nothing, and my power is nothing,
　　I'll bring it here again.

MAURTEEN [*clinging to him*] No.

BRIDGET. Do not leave us.

FATHER HART. O, let me go before it is too late;
　　It is my sin alone that brought it all.

　　　　　　　　[*Singing outside.*]

THE CHILD. I hear them sing, "Come, newly-married bride,
　　Come, to the woods and waters and pale lights."

MARY. I will go with you.

FATHER HART. She is lost, alas!

THE CHILD. [*standing by the door*] But clinging mortal hope must fall from you,
> For we who ride the winds, run on the waves,
> And dance upon the mountains are more light
> Than dewdrops on the banner of the dawn.

MARY. O, take me with you.

SHAWN. Beloved, I will keep you.
> I've more than words, I have these arms to hold you,
> Nor all the faery host, do what they please,
> Shall ever make me loosen you from these arms.

MARY. Dear face! Dear voice!

THE CHILD. Come, newly-married bride.

MARY. I always loved her world—and yet—and yet—

THE CHILD. White bird, white bird, come with me, little bird.

MARY. She calls me!

THE CHILD. Come with me, little bird.

[*Distant dancing figures appear in the wood.*]

MARY. I can hear songs and dancing.

SHAWN. Stay with me.

MARY. I think that I would stay—and yet—and yet—

THE CHILD. Come, little bird, with crest of gold.'

MARY [*very softly.*] And yet—

THE CHILD. Come, little bird with silver feet!

    [*Mary Bruin dies, and the Child goes.*]

SHAWN. She is dead!

BRIDGET. Come from that image; body and soul are gone
    You have thrown your arms about a drift of leaves,
    Or bole of an ash-tree changed into her image.

FATHER HART. Thus do the spirits of evil snatch their prey,
    Almost out of the very hand of God;
    And day by day their power is more and more,
    And men and women leave old paths, for pride
    Comes knocking with thin knuckles on the heart.

    [*Outside there are dancing figures, and it may be a white bird, and many voices singing.*]

The wind blows out of the gates of the day,
The wind blows over the lonely of heart,
And the lonely of heart is withered away;
While the faeries dance in a place apart,
Shaking their milk-white feet in a ring,
Tossing their milk-white arms in the air;
For they hear the wind laugh and murmur and sing
Of a land where even the old are fair,
And even the wise are merry of tongue;
But I heard a reed of Coolaney say—

'When the wind has laughed and murmured and sung,
The lonely of heart is withered away.'

THE END

Lightning Source UK Ltd.
Milton Keynes UK
UKOW051802160812

197648UK00001B/39/P